mnm2

minimalist interiors

mnm2
minimalist interiors

Author : LAURA O'BRYAN

Graphic design : MANEL PERET

Production : JUANJO RODRÍGUEZ NOVEL

Copyright © 2004 for worldwide edition

Atrium Group de ediciones y publicaciones, S.L.

Ganduxer, 112, 2ª pl.

08022 Barcelona

Tel.: + 34 932 540 099

Fax: + 34 932 118 139

e-mail: atrium@atriumgroup.org

www.atriumbooks.com

ISBN : 84-96099-47-4

Dep. Legal: B-9856-04

Printed in Spain

Grabasa, S.L.

SUMMARY

INTRODUCTION

An error frequently made is to identify minimalism exclusively by the color white or to identify emptiness by a lack of content. Our intention has been to include projects in this book that demonstrate this to be an error and show homes that have come to reflect a spontaneity in their interiors as a result of simplification and which find their virtue in geometric simplicity and austerity.

In minimalism, what is important is the naked beauty of the moment. It seeks a height of expressiveness with a minimum of ornamentation and gives particular importance to the fluidity of light and space. As a result, the outstanding feature of these interiors is the intrinsic quality of the materials used and the textures that stand out thanks to the special way light falls on the surfaces. In reality, it deals with a complex process of doing away with all that is superfluous as a reaction against the artificiality that goes along with the present materialistic tendency to accumulate all sorts of unnecessary things that rapidly become obsolete. This, consequently, leads to an obsession with reduction and leaves no more than the indispensable on view, nothing more than the essential. Everything else is unnecessary.

Minimalism in interior design has gone beyond fashion and tendency and has become a new philosophy of life which seeks clean vital spaces in which we can feel the life force of the day to day.

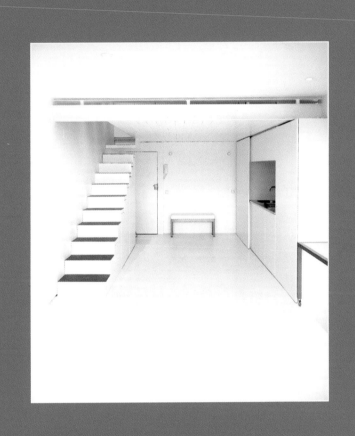

Architects: ARCHIKUBIK

Photographer: EUGENI PONS

Location: BARCELONA, SPAIN

Completion date: 2001

Surface area: 130 m²

MULTI-PURPOSE SPACE

How can you create different ambiences within a large empty space without loss of contact among the different areas of a loft, for example? This team of architects has achieved this by means of solutions that are characterized, on the one hand, by their flexibility and, on the other, by their transparency and which offer the inhabitants of this home a variety of arrangements to meet each and every necessity they may have.

As a result, the space can be arranged as a large open volume or converted into various independent areas with no more than the movement of a hand. The element used for this transformation is a large red sliding panel that crosses the entire home suspended from a metal rail and allows the areas to be separated or freely arranged in different ways. Also, as this panel is the only colored element in the residence, it creates an interesting visual contrast against the white background and becomes the center of attention. The tables, the kitchen modules and storage containers are movable pieces designed by the architects themselves and which can be moved from one place to another or which can even take on different functions when the home is transformed.

Another resource used to achieve the aforementioned flexibility is the cube that separates the night zone from the day zone. This, like the sliding door, does not reach the ceiling so as to intensify the sensation of amplitude, to allow the wooden beams to be seen and to let natural light flood into the entire home. The cube contains the bathroom. This can be accessed from the bedroom or from the living area through sliding doors that allow the three zones to be connected or to enjoy complete independence. The total transparency of the elements that make up the bathroom stands out and gives it an almost weightless appearance.

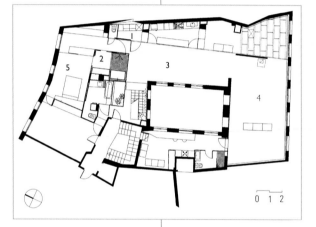

0 1 2

1. Kitchen
2. Bathroom
3. Dining area
4. Living area
5. Bedroom

Versatility defines practically all of the elements
in this home such as the red panel in
DM wood that communicates
or separates, or the table that can function
as a work surface, dining table
or study desk

The bathroom stands out for its complete transparency.
Its presence goes practically unnoticed as it integrates
into the decoration of the area from which
it is viewed

Architects: PIERRE HOET/IN STORE SA

Photographer: STELLA ROTGER

Location: BRUSSELS, BELGIUM

Completion date: 2000

Surface area: 160 m²

THE ATTRACTION OF OPPOSITES

This loft situated in the center of Brussels is a clear example of an industrial building converted into a residence. The architect has made an effort to maintain the spirit of this old leather workshop. The original steel columns of the construction have been kept and the open spatial structure maintained. Only the bedroom and bathroom form an independent element within the space of the residence.

Colors and materials unify the large central body in which the kitchen, living area, dining area and studio are found. These elements form a harmonious whole that has been generated on the basis of contrasts. The coldness of the stainless steel in the kitchen is compensated for by the warmth of the holm oak wood used for flooring and by the carpets made in natural fibers. The rustic wooden tables and chairs and the antiques acquire a renewed importance in juxtaposition with the large number of contemporary artworks that are exhibited throughout the home. The choice of a color scheme based on light tones manages to integrate these contrasts which are perceived as forming part of an overall order.

The light, which is distributed uniformly throughout the space, also contributes to the unified perception of the whole. This loft enjoys the privilege of having a large number of entrances for natural light. As a result, there is not a single corner that is darker than another. In addition to these generously sized windows which give onto the street there is also a large skylight in the central space through which sunlight floods in and modifies the atmosphere in this area as the sun changes its position. The bedroom has its own source of light thanks to an interior patio to which it has direct access.

The respective qualities of the contemporary and traditional materials counterbalance one another and coexist in perfect harmony

Light plays a leading role in this home.
A large number of entrances for natural light
are available: the windows, the skylight
and the interior patio closed off
by French windows

The contemporary art and antique furniture offer
an interesting contrast which gives personality
to the different ambiences

Architects: LUIS CUARTAS

Collaborator: GUILLERMO ARIAS

Photographer: EDUARDO CONSUEGRA

Location: BOGOTÁ, COLOMBIA

Completion date: 2000

Surface area: 90 m²

FIRE AND WATER

The complete reform undertaken during this project provides a good example of how the most of available space has been made. The starting point was an old house situated in the center of Bogotá from which two new residences have been obtained. The almost symmetrical floor plan of the original house has enabled it to be divided into two equal areas in each of which one of the architects who undertook the refurbishing has established his or her own private residence. Evidently, each of the areas reflects its owner's personal conception of architectural space and responds to his or her ideas and necessities.

In this case, the residence occupies the space where the kitchen, bathroom and dining room were previously found. To make the most of the available square meters, the idea of a circular distribution that connects all of the areas, without interruption, and does away with entrance halls and passages has been pursued. As a result, the different areas flow together and this strengthens the sensation of amplitude.

From the entrance, a visit to the residence can be undertaken from either the left or the right. The first option takes us directly to the kitchen that has been resolved in the form of a U and furnished with the same type of made to measure containers that are found in the rest of the home. The second option, invites us to follow the line marked by an original bench-container until we arrive at one of the most surprising pieces of the house: a piece of construction work that integrates a bath and a fireplace. Fire and water set side by side. The textures and colors seem to emphasis this union. The steel, the glass and the gray of the cement play in favor of the water; the wood, the reddish tones of the bricks and the intense red of the concrete floor reflect the warmth of the fire.

Previous floor plan

Present floor plan

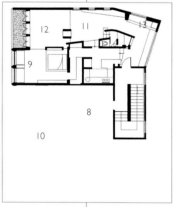

1. Kitchen
2. Bathroom
3. Dining area
4. Terrace
5. Bedroom
6. Child's bedroom
7. Hall
8. Kitchen

9. Wardrobe
10. Room
11. Living area
12. Terrace
13. Bathroom

0 1 2

The bathroom has become the central axis
of the apartment's distribution.
It is slightly raised with respect to the
other areas, which again strengthens
its condition of being an
independent space

The made to measure furniture, which is multi-use
and incorporated into the architecture
of the residence, helps make the most of the
available space

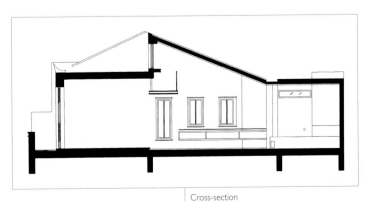

Cross-section

The kitchen has been laid out in the form of a U
so that the work surface is located just below
the elongated skylight that allows the area
to be flooded by natural light

Architects: MANUEL OCAÑA DEL VALLE

Collaborator: CELIA LÓPEZ AGUADO, LAURA ROJO

Photographer: ALFONSO POSTIGO

Location: MADRID, SPAIN

Completion date: 2000

Surface area: 85 m²

A NEW ORDER

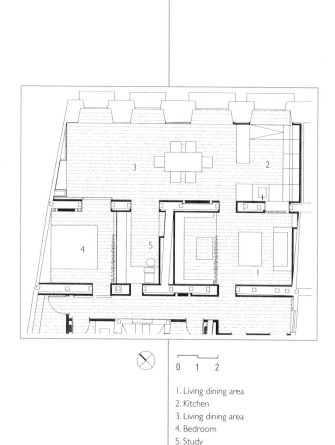

0 1 2

1. Living dining area
2. Kitchen
3. Living dining area
4. Bedroom
5. Study

Over the base of an old apartment in the center of Madrid, the priority in this refurbishing has been that of freeing the interior space and giving it a new regular order. The original residence responded to the old criteria of distributing space into a number of separate compartments which hindered movement within the interior.

Consequently, the first step was to tear down the partition walls and leave a large space like «a blank page» in which a new order of orthogonal structure could be created. This large space was divided lengthways into two equal parts which have received different treatments. The first is a completely open space shared by the common or day zones, which is to say the kitchen, the living area and the dining area. The second half has been divided into three different ambiences – the bedroom, the study and a more intimate room - which are communicated thanks to the large glazed surfaces of the central zone occupied by the study which permits a visual continuity through the different areas of the residence. By these means, the spatial amplitude of a loft has been obtained without having to give up the intimacy offered by more traditional spaces separated by partition walls. What is more, better use of the available space has been made as, for example, in the study zone where shelves have been fitted practically all around the perimeter that have permitted the creation of a small library.

The choice of aluminum for all of the fixed furnishings - such as the cooker, the bathtub, and the large study table - of glass to separate the ambiences along with the dominance of the color white give this loft a style of great contemporaneity which is, at the same time, timeless. This sensation is strengthened by the presence, in the living area, of two of the most emblematic designs of the 20th century: the chaise-longue by Le Corbusier and the chairs by Eero Saarinen.

The transparency of the glass manages to separate
the most intimate ambiences without
disturbing the visual communication between them

The star of the kitchen and bathroom is aluminum.
It gives these areas an aspect
of great contemporaneity

Architects: HUGH BROUGHTON ARCHITECTS

Photographer: CARLOS DOMÍNGUEZ

Location: GLOUCESTERSHIRE, UK

Completion date: 1999-2000

Surface area: 90 m²

A MULTIFUNCTIONAL RECTANGLE

With the help of three small walls, this oblong, which was previously a dance-hall in a small palace constructed at the beginning of the 20th century, has been transformed into a home with four different ambiences.

These three architectural volumes serve, in addition to distributing the space and limiting the zone occupied by each area, as pieces of furniture that can be used in different ways: as a bookcase in the living area, to accommodate the shower in the bathroom and as a wardrobe in the dressing area while also serving as a bed head. These walls become the principal elements of the residence and articulate the space. This dominance is strengthened by the fact that the lateral areas have been left completely free of obstacles which reinforces their presence.

The architect himself has also designed the rest of the furniture. In this way, a unity within the living space has been achieved along with a continuity, so as to say, of the philosophy that dominates the project: the purity of line, the elimination of whatever superfluous detail, the quality of the materials, simplicity as a source of inspiration, the importance of light and, above all, an atmosphere of complete serenity. To rephrase these words, the residence is a good example of well-understood minimalism.

The fact that the four ambiences obtain a total independence from each other, in spite of being separated in a minimal way, is surprising. In a visual way, this differentiation is helped by the flooring in the bathroom where the cold appearance of the ground, reminiscent of stone, contrasts with the old parquet flooring with its classical spiked design.

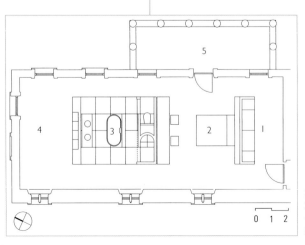

1. Dressing room
2. Bedroom
3. Bathroom
4. Living area
5. Terrace

0 1 2

Leaving the lateral spaces
of the oblong almost empty,
the presence of the small walls,
which acquire almost sculptural properties,
is strengthened

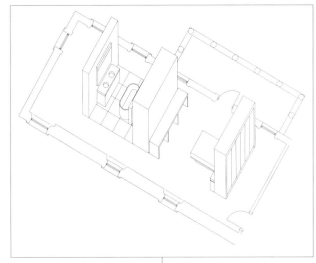

Axonometric perspective

The channels for water and electricity
have been hidden within the structure of the walls,
thus, freeing the space

Architect: ANTONIO FIOL

Photographer: STELLA ROTGER

Location Location: MAJORCA, SPAIN

Completion date: 2000-2001

Surface area: 70 m²

AN ETERNAL SPRING

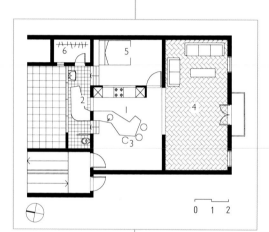

1. Kitchen
2. Bathroom
3. Dining area
4. Living area
5. Bedroom
6. Wardrobe

This apartment, located in the city of Palma de Mallorca, gives off freshness and discharges spontaneity from all of its corners. After the lengthy refurbishing carried out, it is as if the interiors have awoken from a long hibernation and flowered in a new space full of life, of light and undulating lines that echo nature's organic forms.

The new distribution communicates the spaces amongst themselves by establishing a circular route which invites us to follow the beautiful stone-topped table in serpentine like forms, which complement the curves of the built-in bathtub found three steps higher, and to continue to the bedroom and living area where the route starts all over again. Even the physically closed areas communicate with each other. This is the case of the kitchen and the bedroom which are connected by means of a horizontal glass window that crosses the common wall.

The presence of nature is felt not only through the organicism of the forms, but also by the outstanding presence possessed by the flowers and plants that are integrated into the furnishings themselves. This is the case of the dining table into which, in addition to the sink, a small metal vase has been inserted, not to mention the built-in sofa that extends laterally forming large flowerpots and contrasting the gray of the concrete with the green of the plants.

The almost complete absence of furniture, apart from that integrated into the architecture, creates a completely unencumbered space which strengthens the springlike sensation of freshness. The only thing that stands out on the wall of the dining area is the well-known shelf designed by Ron Arad that contributes to foment the omnipresence of curved forms.

Un espace dressé au coeur, c'est-à-dire de l'idée dans l'élément abstrait de la pensée, chaque matin repris en rêve, et chaque soir aban

The only touch of color is that provided
by nature, by the flowers, the fruit and
the plants that splash color into all
of the corners

A platform has been built into the living area
that serves as much as the base for the sofa
as to integrate nature into the very architecture
of the residence

En Architecture, j'aime la simplicité ; de même, en cuisine.

En Architecture, j'aime la simplicité ; de même, en cuisine.

The bathroom has been constructed in a place
that was previously an interior patio and, as a result,
receives a great deal of light that spreads to the rest
of the areas

Architects: STEPHEN QUINN & ELISE OVANESSOFF

Photographer: JORDI MIRALLES

Location: LONDON, UK

Completion date: 2000-2001

Surface area: 60 m²

LIVING IN AN OLD GEORGIAN HOUSE

The architects have converted this old reception area of a Georgian house, constructed two hundred years ago, into a comfortable modern apartment adapted to present-day necessities. The only elements that are reminiscent of the house's begotten splendor and which give a light noble touch to the general atmosphere created in the new space are the large windows, the plasterwork on the ceilings and the beautiful fireplace with its carved wooden frame.

The residence has been divided into two different parts. On one side, there is a large zone divided into living area, dining area and kitchen and, then, the other side, the more intimate zone which has been fragmented and divided into three pieces: bedroom, dressing area and bathroom. The interiors have been resolved by the balanced combination of the only two colors used: the white of the walls and upholstery and the chocolate color, almost black, of the furniture in wenge wood and the raised floor. The result is one of elegance and harmony. Whitish tones have also been chosen for the kitchen fittings which almost manage to go unperceived.

In the bedroom, the only colored element of the entire house is found. This is a large sliding door in eye-catching white, blue and green stripes that separates the dressing area from the rest of the space and manages to stand out from its monochromatic surroundings and to almost take on a life of its own that suggests it could be contemplated as if it were a painting hung on the wall of a museum. A simple bed in natural wood, which incorporates four large drawers in a rustic style, is the outstanding feature of this space. The bathroom, accessed by the stairs, occupies a small space designed down to the last millimeter.

1. Kitchen
2. Bathroom
3. Living dining area
4. Dressing room
5. Bedroom

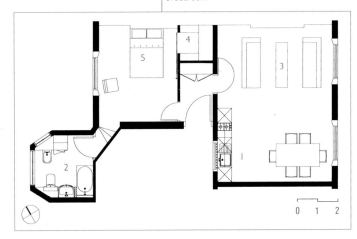

0 1 2

The combination of the whites and chocolate colors leads
to an atmosphere that is balanced and harmonious
as well as being slightly austere. This effect is strengthened
by the virtual absence of decorative objects

The sliding door that separates the bedroom
from the living area represents the only daring use
of colors in the entire residence. It brings
a dose of freshness and cheerfulness to the home

Architect: MANUEL OCAÑA DEL VALLE

Collaborators: CELIA LÓPEZ AGUADO, LAURA ROJO

Photographer: LUIS ASÍN

Location: MADRID, SPAIN

Completion date: 2001

Surface area: 85 m²

ORDER AS OPPOSED TO CHAOS

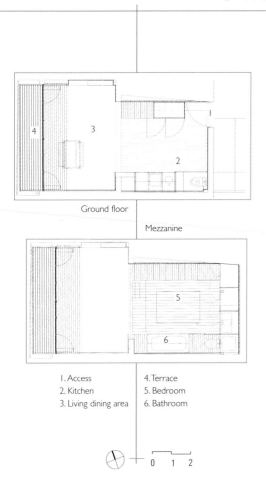

Ground floor

Mezzanine

1. Access
2. Kitchen
3. Living dining area
4. Terrace
5. Bedroom
6. Bathroom

0   1   2

At first sight this residence located in a densely populated neighborhood of Madrid seems to be an empty white box. A much closer examination is required to discover the details hidden in its structure which provide the necessary conditions that make it fit to live in. The decision to integrate almost all of the furnishings and services into the architecture of the apartment itself corresponds to two of the basic requisites of the refurbishing project: to make the most of the limited space available and to create a bubble of order and vitality in which to take refuge from the noise and chaos of the urban surroundings.

The starting point was a small 30-m²-storage area situated below the sloping roof of an old residential building. The highest point measured 4.5m, so the first move was to construct a mezzanine in order to gain another 8.5m² of usable space. The lower floor is a space that offers a great flexibility given its ability to adapt to the activity being carried out at any time. When you are cooking, everything becomes the kitchen. When you eat, everything becomes a dining room and when you relax, it all becomes a living room. The absence of elements that define the ambiences and the conformity in coloring and use of textures make these simple transformations possible.

One of the resources that stands out the most is the raised area that prolongs the terrace into the interior of the living space. In addition to fusing the exterior with the interior, when the folding French windows are open, it also doubles the size of the terrace. As far as the interior is concerned, it becomes a bench to sit on when eating thanks to the ingenious made to measure table with a form that adapts to the situation.

Luminosity and transparencies also prevail on the first floor where the bedroom, dressing area and bathroom are located. The final result achieves order over the frenzy of the capital.

A suspended wooden box prolongs the terrace
and becomes an area of transition
between a chaotic exterior and an interior full
of calmness

Longitudinal sections

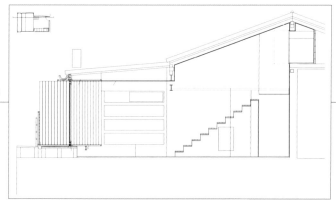
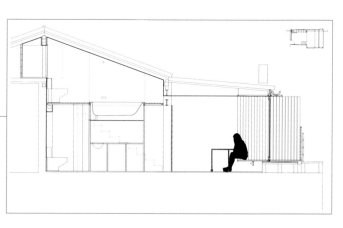

The limited space has made it necessary to make the most
of the available surface area. The built-in shelves
or the wardrobe hidden in the space under the stairs
are two good solutions

A translucent glass screen
that follows the inclination of the ceiling serves
to separate the bedroom
and bathroom

Architects: GARY CHANG/EDGE (HK) LTD.

Collaborators: CHENG GUNN, WONG CHUNG WAI

Photographer: ALMOND CHU

Location: HONG KONG, CHINA

Completion date: 2000

Surface area: 30 m²

A PLAY ON CURTAINS

This project presents new examples of space saving solutions. In only 30m², previously shared by a large family, the architect has managed to integrate all of the functions necessary to establish his own residence.

To achieve flexible ambiences was, in this case, the unavoidable proposition. In a small area organized around the main source of natural light, there would have to be room for the bedroom, living room, studio and video room. This has been achieved by using movable furniture, carefully studied environmental lighting and lightweight separating elements such as the white curtains. Around this central nucleus, a metal shelving system has been installed. This serves as general storage space and contains an audio video library, all of which is kept out of sight thanks to the curtains. According to what sort of activity is being carried out, certain curtains are opened while others are closed. This leads to the creation of different atmospheres. Underneath the shelves, fluorescent lamps, which give a dreamy aspect to the home along with a sensation of weightlessness, have been installed. The changes in lighting also indicate the changes in use, the nocturnal activities taking over from those of the day.

A block of cherry wood acts as a backbone and combines the different ambiences. It has become the only visually solid element in the residence and stands out for its versatility. It contains and hides the video projector, the refrigerator and washing machine as well as acting as a partition between the kitchen and bathroom. Every detail has been carefully studied so as to make the most of the space available while a certain sensation of amplitude has been achieved not only as far as movement is concerned, but on a visual level as well.

1. Access
2. Kitchen
3. Bathroom
4. Living area and bedroom
5. Study
6. Wardrobe

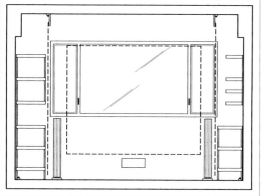

Cross section of the living area

The area of the window becomes a projection screen
for videos and the television. With drawn curtains
and suitable illumination, the space is transformed
into a small cinema in which free time
can be enjoyed

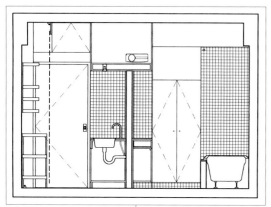

Cross section of bathroom and kitchen

In this tiny bathroom, the faucets and contemporary
sanitaryware, the small format ceramic tiling in white
and the partition wall that has been substituted
by a lightweight curtain manage to integrate, in comfort,
all of the elements that are necessary
in this area

Just one space fulfills the functions of living room,
bedroom, study and video room thanks to the carefully
studied distribution of the metal shelves
and the use of the curtains

Longitudinal sections

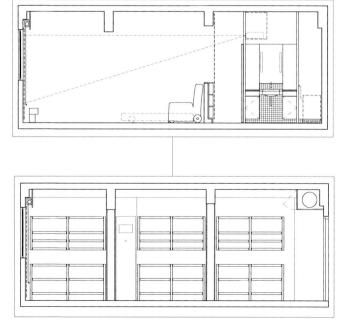

Architects: BRIAN MA SIY ARCHITECTS

Photographer: JORDI MIRALLES

Location: LONDON, UK

Completion date: 1996

Surface area: 80 m²

BACK TO SCHOOL

This apartment in London was previously the ground floor foyer of an old school from which the classrooms were accessed. With the refurbishing process completed, it has become the home of an architect and has replaced school discipline with a luminous and contemporary space.

The residence is spread over two floors. The clear open space of the ground floor is shared by the living area and the kitchen while, upstairs, the bedrooms and bathroom are found. All of the decorative elements stand out for simplicity of line and create an atmosphere which is at the same tome austere and comfortable. The two ambiences on the lower floor are delimited visually by means of a stainless steel sheet, 350cm long and 100cm wide, which is supported by an arrangement of furniture units. This counter fulfills various functions: it is used as a kitchen worktop, kitchen sink and dining table.

The cooker has been manufactured by the German firm Bulthaup and stands out for its contemporary and functional design. Some large cupboards which combine laminates in cobalt blue with stainless steel hide the electrical appliances and kitchen accessories while introducing a touch of color, which breaks the uniformity of white, into the atmosphere. The living area has been resolved with two white sofas set face to face, a collection of watercolors and a low piece of furniture that runs all along the wall.

One of the most outstanding corners of the apartment is where the staircase that gives access to the upper floor has been located. In addition to the design of the staircase, which manages to give the sensation of lightness thanks to a combination of steel and wooden treads without risers, the large built-in bookcase is of particular interest. This makes use of the space created by the stairwell and covers the wall from the bottom of the lower floor to the top of the higher.

The whiteness of the walls and the seating furniture
along with the stainless steel of the kitchen worktop
and cooking zone manage to increase the luminosity
of this space

The steel counter is the outstanding feature
of this space as much for its contemporary design
as for its great versatility

The bedroom and bathroom stand out for
their simplicity and shared color scheme. In the bedroom,
the color of the furniture has been unified with that
of the wooden flooring which has helped create
a compact unit

■

Architect: Jonathan Clark

Photographer: Jan Baldwin

Location: London, UK

Completion date: 1995

Surface area: 140 m²

Everlasting elegance

The architect Jonathan Clark has converted this old house into his own residence. The principal refurbishing work consisted in eliminating the old partition walls and low ceilings. The result is a large space in which the differentiated areas are well communicated, but which, at the same time, manage to maintain their independence.

The large central space is shared by the kitchen, dining area and living area. These areas are special in the sense that they can be open or closed according to the preferences of the moment. For example, the kitchen, which is integrated into the dining area, can be discretely closed off when desired as if it were a cupboard. Also, the dining area itself can be separated from the living area with the simple movement of closing a sliding door which is found between the two areas and which, due to its dimensions, becomes a movable partition.

In the decoration, the noble materials and some of the most recognizable and immortal creations of the last century stand out: the «Swan» seats and the mythical chair «3107», which are still being produced almost 50 years after their conception, from the great Danish designer Arne Jacobsen. A spacious passage leads to the bathroom which has been completely done out in small ceramic tiles and divided into two zones (one with a shower and the other with a bath). The bedroom consists of a large piece of made to measure furniture that fulfills various functions. The central part, which acts as a bedhead, frames the window in addition to being a support for the reading lamps and built-in spotlights. The sides and upper part enclose a practical discretely hidden wardrobe. The base of the bed, having been made in the same wood, complements and completely integrates with the rest of the room.

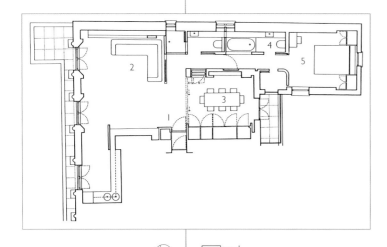

0 1 2

1. Access
2. Living area
3. Kitchen with dining area
4. Bathroom
5. Bedroom

The bathroom has been located in the
broad passage and divided into two zones:
one in which a shower has been incorporated
and the other in which there is a bathtub situated
over a small raised area and which acquires
sculptural properties

A large piece of furniture, which occupies the entire wall,
fulfills all of the functions of the bedroom: bed base,
wardrobe, bedhead and support for lighting.
The florescent lamps that have been incorporated into
its base give the impression of weightlessness
to the bed

Architects: BLOCKARCHITECTURE

Photographer: LEON CHEW

Location: LONDON, UK

Completion date: 2001

Surface area: 85 m^2

A WOODEN BOX

This top floor London apartment organized over a rectangular plan has been transformed into a large wooden box in which the different uses of the dwelling have been distributed. In fact, the architects commissioned for this refurbishing project based their intervention on a design that has attempted to imitate the concept of a tree house. It is a wooden square that emerges out of the space creating a protective environment that is in contact with its natural surroundings.

The bedroom was made in this way: a platform was suspended in the air with walls formed by panels made up of strips of iroko wood that creates the illusion of a house within a house and which establishes a slight visual contact between the different areas, but maintains privacy at the same time. When a greater connection between the spaces is desired, the central part of the wooden panel can be opened which becomes, in this way, a large window that looks out onto the exterior world.

The kitchen has been resolved in the same way, with the same system of wooden strips. These cover the lower cupboard units of a central island which acts as a discrete decorative element and differentiates ambiences. White predominates in this markedly minimalist space in which cupboards designed with essential lines and lacquered in white that almost reach the ceiling go practically unnoticed.

At night, The light that filters through from the inside of the wooden panels creates some greatly dramatic effects. The "«tree house», in which the bedroom is located, seems to float in the air as a result of the light that comes out from under its base.

Wood is the outstanding feature
of this interior inspired
in tree houses

The module in iroko wood, which protects the bedroom
from the exterior, can be opened when desired so
as to enjoy the views that are contemplated
from the terrace

A wooden platform has also been installed on the
terrace which establishes a visual continuity between
the interior and exterior

Architect: SIMON CORDER

Photographer: JORDI MIRALLES

Location: LONDON, UK

Completion date: 2001

Surface area: 30 m²

A GLASS LIVING ROOM IN THE GARDEN

This project for an extension to a nineteenth century London house is a good example of how traditional architecture can be fused with contemporary aesthetics. The new owner wished to make the most of a piece of adjoining unused land and, consequently, installed this large metal-framed glass box that resembles a large greenhouse.

In this new space annexed to the older construction, a luminous living room and dining area have been installed which are midway between inside and outside. From this new space, it is possible to enjoy the short afternoons typical of British winters to the maximum. This glass box can be entered by any of three doors: two of which allow for direct access from the outside – through doors in iroko wood that equal the facade in height and break the symmetrical continuity of the glass walls -, and the last door which connects with the interior. The decoration has been resolved with a concrete floor stained white and a few simple pieces of furniture in beech wood. Among these pieces the sofas with rectangular wooden bases and the emblematic chairs "Wishbone" designed in 1950 by Hans J. Wegner, one of the most important representatives of Danish organic design which is enjoying a strong comeback in the 21st century, stand out.

The illumination plays a fundamental role in this new space stolen from the garden. The natural light is the absolute star during the day. However, the artificial lighting takes over at night given that the sofas and auxiliary tables have warm-toned fluorescent lamps incorporated in their bases which create a diffused light that brings a certain fantasy and makes the space appear as if it were a magic lantern in the garden.

A corridor with stone walls and floor and wooden beams
establishes various transitory spaces
between the interior of the old house
and the new glazed living room

The strategic collocation of artificial light takes on
a great importance in the definition of this space which
is transformed into a make-believe world and
which illuminates the garden as if it were a large lantern

Architect: MARK GUARD

Photographer: MARK GUARD

Location: LONDON, UK

Completion date: 1996

Surface area: 95 m²

A PEACEFUL SPACE

Absolute peace reigns over the atmosphere of this apartment with almost monastic aesthetics. The main area is a large empty space that offers extraordinary versatility for transformation. It can be arranged and rearranged for different uses according to the necessities of each and every moment.

The kitchen stands out in this space. It has been designed in stainless steel modules divided into three bodies that integrate into the architecture itself and can go completely unnoticed once the folding doors that have been inserted between the modules have been closed. A folding top fulfills the function of dining table which is stored completely out of sight when not in use. In this way, this ambience has the attribute of disappearing when it is not required. The master bedroom, the guestroom and dressing room occupy three independent modules which are also separated by movable partition walls that contribute to the total flexibility of the home.

Another eye-catching element is the six-meter-long stainless steel worktop that divides the central space down the middle and sections the thick wall that carries the installations and a storage space which, as the majority of things in this residence, is conveniently hidden. This steel table extends visually up to the washbasin thanks to a glass screen that separates the two ambiences in such a way that they appear to form a whole. Next to the washbasin, in the middle of this space, a shower with sculptural properties and which is separated from the access zone by means of a simple curved translucent glass screen emerges.

The majority of the functions and uses of this apartment
can be hidden away out of sight according to the interests
of the moment. As a result, it is a space that offers
extraordinary versatility when a change of use
is called for and in which the most absolute order
clearly predominates

Architects: VINCENT JAMES & PAUL YAGGIE

Photographer: DON F. WONG

Location Location: WISCONSIN, US

Completion date: 1996

Surface area: 700 m²

A PLAY ON VOLUMES

The construction project for this residence was based on the concept of a cube and a play on the spaces created by the intersection of volumes. The house creates different architectural situations that occur between its component bodies that are similar to wooden boxes. This treatment responds to the clients' desire to adapt the construction to a concept that they define as «type/variant''. This idea comes from the impression given by, for example, a butterfly collection in which the variations established based on clear classifying principles magnify the particularities of each specimen.

In the same way, in this intersection of cubes in which each one has its own determined proportion, orientation and natural illumination, the play between similarities and differences manages to create a collection of interrelated spaces which give a great aesthetic impact in addition to being highly functional. Each new orientation offers a new overall view of the surroundings and each new angle created by an intersection not only leads to a new semi-closed exterior space, but to a quiet intimate interior one as well.

The interiors are of a great simplicity as the rooms, and also the patios, have been conceived as simple spaces that are to come to life through daily use and with the passing of time. The materials used themselves, wood and natural stone, become the principal decorative elements and manage to transmit an immediate sensation of warmth. Also of interest are the facades that have been covered in sheet copper and stone which have been fitted in different textures and have been left untreated so as to age with the passing of time in a natural way.

Elevation

0 1 2

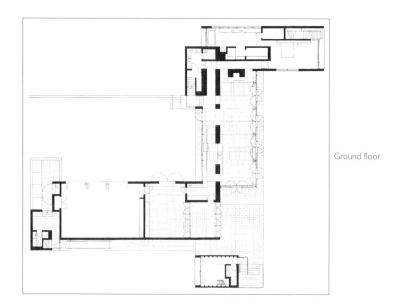

Ground floor

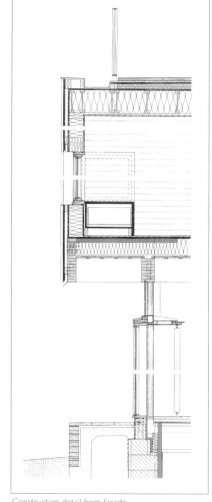

Construction detail from facade

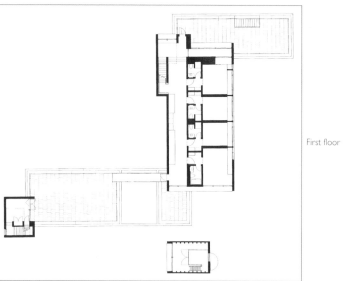

First floor

0 1 2

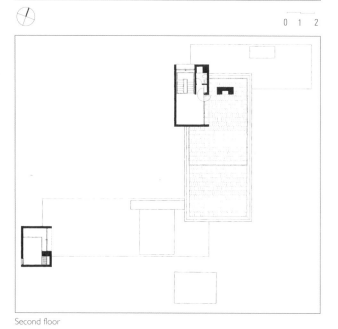

Second floor

The texture and warmth of the varnished wood
and natural stone that cover the floors,
walls and ceilings are the principal, and only,
decoration in the interior
of this house

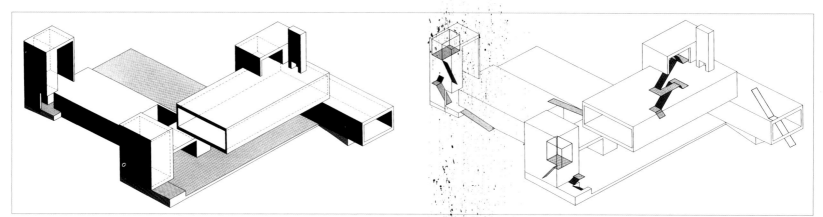

Details of the fireplace

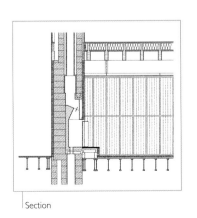

Section

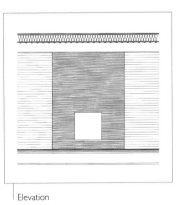

Elevation

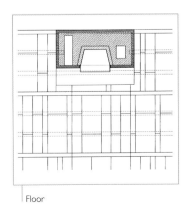

Floor

Architect: MONEO BROCK

Photographer: JORDI MIRALLES

Location: NEW YORK, US

Completion date: 2000

Surface area: 150 m²

THE RECOVERY OF AN OLD WAREHOUSE

This 150-m² loft in New York corresponds to the original movement of recovering old warehouses and abandoned factories and converting them into residences in response to a new lifestyle that broke away from traditional taboos. In this particular case, the starting point was a cold abandoned warehouse with nothing more than concrete walls, some thick pillars and a few windows oriented to the east.

After the refurbishing process, not a trace of its dismal origins remains. Even the pillars have received a new look. The result is a space that has been transformed into a contemporary and luminous residence in which the different spaces communicate one with the other with the greatest of fluidity or by means of movable divisions formed by sliding glass doors. The furniture has been chosen for its modern design and, above all, for its comfort and spatial fluidity. It plays on a contrast between black and white. The presence of one of the most renown icons of 20th century designs stands out in the living area: the standard lamp "Arco" by Pier and Achille Castiglioni in brilliant stainless steel that harmonizes perfectly with the legs of the sofas and central table. The explosion of color in the work by Amanda Guest that receives the visitor upon entry also stands out.

The kitchen is separated visually from the living area by a marble-topped counter which, all at once, serves as sink, breakfast/snack table and storage unit. The wall in the background has been completely covered in small ceramic tiles in various tones of gray that blend into the overall appearance along with the translucent glass doors of the cupboards and stainless steel appliances.

The furniture and decorative accessories
have been carefully chosen as much
for their timeless contemporaneity
as for their functionality

The bedroom stands out for its absolute simplicity.
A simple wooden bed of a slight oriental influence
is all there is to be found here

Architect: KAR-HWA HO

Photographer: BJÖRG

Location: NEW YORK, US

Completion date: 1999

Surface area: 225 m²

SYMMETRICAL SET

One of the main objectives of the refurbishing that was undertaken on this residence was to free the existing space from its classical divisions and to unify the different ambiences in such a way as to transmit order and serenity. The final result corresponds to the contemporary style of residence which is divided into two broad zones: one for the day that comprises the living area, the dining area and the kitchen, and the night zone, with a more intimate atmosphere, made up of the bedroom and bathroom.

In general, both the furniture and the chosen color scheme have helped create a discrete environment in which a visual calmness based on the symmetry of the design predominates. The pieces of furniture seem to have been arranged in such a way so as to obtain a perfect equilibrium in which not a single element overshadows another nor breaks the harmony of the group.

Starting from the kitchen, in which a storage unit of an unusual height and that also serves as a separator of ambiences stands out, the different groups of furniture are arranged in an ordered way: firstly, we find a dining table in wenge wood with six chairs upholstered in vanilla-colored leather. Next, seats designed with straight lines arranged in parallel to each other and opposite a sofa from the same range with the same upholstery in a light olive color. Closing the living area and separating a group of chairs from the wall full of cupboards, a divan, upholstered in beige-colored leather, is found. All of the pieces seem to have a location, a color and a texture which all seem to have been studied in the greatest of detail and which establish an interrelationship amongst themselves of such a nature that if just one of the pieces were eliminated, our entire perception of the space would change.

Even in the bedroom, the same colors and textures
that predominate in the principal area of the residence
have been used. In this way, the sensation of balance
is not interrupted when moving from one area to another

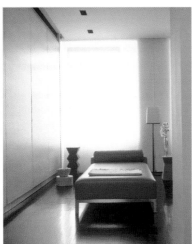

Architect: KAR-HWA HO

Photographer: BJÖRG

Location: NEW YORK, US

Completion date: 1996

Surface area: 160 m²

LOFT IN NEW YORK

This is a new example of the contemporary concept of the home divided into two large zones: the principal zone consists of the kitchen, with a free-standing storage unit that separates ambiences, the dining area and the living area to which, in this case, a large working area, which brings the old concept of an office up to date, has been added. On the other side, we find the more private zone that accommodates the bedrooms and bathroom, which, as in this case, tends to be separated from the rest of the residence by movable elements such as sliding doors.

On crossing the threshold, the visitor is received by two examples of the emblematic chair "Zig-Zag" designed in 1934 by Gerrit Thomas Rietveld who manages to stamp on his furniture a magical synthesis between the design of the article and the architectural space itself. This synthesis is highlighted by the sunlight that filters in from behind a false ceiling. A variety of materials have been successfully combined in the principal zone: wood, steel, glass and leather have been used in just the right doses to create a relaxing atmosphere. The vaulted brick ceiling, the only visible indication of this residence's origins, stands out in the living area.

The freestanding kitchen unit has been finished in a stainless steel covering and an acid treated glass front which gives it a great sensation of lightness. As far as the study that is located next to the living area is concerned, the design has managed to make the most of the available space with the use of a series of metal-structured tables with made to measure glass tops. In this zone, another «immortal» chair in the history of design stands out: the swivel chair "LC7" designed in 1927 by Le Corbusier in collaboration with Pierre Jeanneret and Charlotte Perriand.

1. Access
2. Kitchen with dining area
3. Living area
4. Bedrooms
5. Bathroom

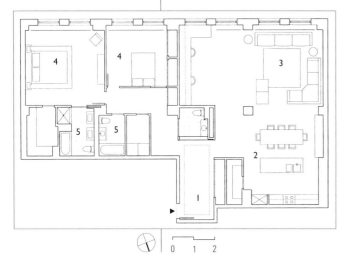

0   1   2

Kitchen, dining area, living area and study share
the same zone. There is no confusion of functions
thanks to the artful way in which the furniture
has been arranged and which visually separates
the different ambiences

The use of transparent glass
in different spaces reduces the sensation of weight
in the overall atmosphere

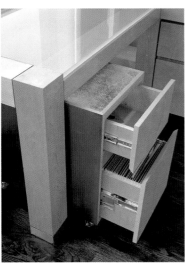

Architects: Cecconi Simone Inc.

Photographer: Joy Von Tiedemann

Location: Toronto, Canada

Completion date: 1999

Surface area: 280 m²

Avant-garde with a past

Avant-garde and nostalgia for the past have been fused in this loft located in an old industrial area of Toronto which, as has occurred in so many other western capitals, has found its physiognomy and function changed thanks to the interest of an emerging social group formed essentially by artists who see an ideal way of stamping a bohemian air, along with freedom, onto their homes in the rehabilitation of old factories.

The large empty spaces, the freedom of movement from one area to another, the firm expression of its industrial origins and a particular passion for recycling are the distinctive features of this loft in which the designers have known how to combine past and present with wisdom. To achieve this integration, the first step was to recover as much of the original structure as possible. As a result, the installations of water and electricity have been left on sight and the original concrete floor and columns restored. On the other hand, most of the furniture has been recycled and given a new function such as the large refrigerator doors or the old steel containers. In the areas that required new furniture, the bathroom and bedroom, it has been specifically designed by the architects themselves so as to ensure that it integrates perfectly with the rest. To complement the overall space, some masterpieces of design have been chosen such as the black chair with high backrest "Hill House" created by Charles R. Mackintosh more than a century ago. In general, the light rustic charm radiated by this residence manages to transmit warmth in spite of its amplitude and the nakedness of the space.

Flexibility is another of the predominating aspects of this residence. This has been achieved thanks to the simple curtains hung from steel bars that can be used to divide the principal area of the loft into three different and intimate ambiences when and as desired.

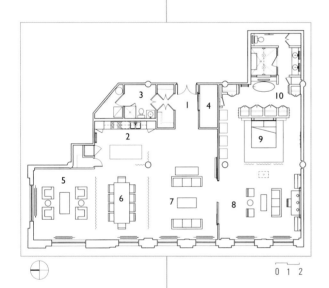

0 1 2

1. Entrance
2. Kitchen
3. Bathroom
4. Cloakroom
5. Living area
6. Dining area
7. Living area
8. Study
9. Bedroom
10. Bathroom

The original characteristics of this modern loft along with the furniture chosen, some of the pieces have been recycled and others are considered to be masterpieces from the history of design, create an atmosphere with a great personality that manages to transmit warmth within this large structure of an industrial origin

The bedroom has been conceived in such a way so
as to offer the maximum of flexibility. The bed is on
wheels which allow it to be moved while the original
roller blind like canopy with adjustable height can be used
to control the degree of intimacy and light desired

Architects: BLOCKARCHITECTURE

Photographer: CHRIS TUBBS

Location: LONDON, UK

Completion date: 1998

Surface area: 175 m²

FREEDOM OF MOVEMENTS

Complete freedom of movement and a non-discriminating treatment of the different domestic functions have been the bases over which the rehabilitation project for this residence has been developed. This follows the underlying philosophy of this particular architectural studio which is that of creating inspiring spaces favorable to creative activities.

Maybe, at first sight, the most surprising thing is the singular way the bathroom zone has been dealt with. The old concept of this being an intimate area has been done away with and it has been shamelessly placed in the middle of the space not only free from enclosures, but also raised on a concrete platform above other elements. The presence of an antique style freestanding bathtub with metal legs in contemporary surroundings also offers an interesting contrast.

So as to obtain an extensive central space free of restrictions, an imposing nine-meter wall was included in the design. The wall, constructed from recycled steel panels, acts as a second skin under which the reception area, a small storeroom, the toilet and a small darkroom for developing photographs are hidden. When completely closed, it gives the impression that the residence is totally isolated from the rest of the world. The kitchen and bathroom have been situated in parallel on the opposite wall achieving, in this way, a large intermediate zone clear of obstacles that allows for a great diversity of different activities to be carried out. As a result, the residence is a large versatile open space that is ideal for artistic creation and for the free flowing of ideas just as intended by the initial rehabilitation scheme.

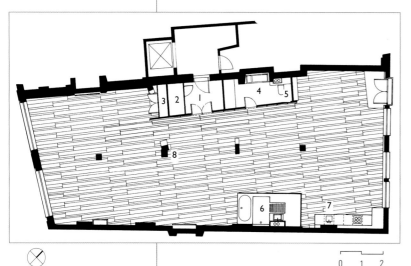

1. Entrance
2. Storeroom
3. Clothes' cupboard
4. Darkroom
5. Toilet
6. Bathroom
7. Kitchen
8. Multi-purpose space

0   1   2

By situating the diverse domestic functions against
the walls, a large central area free of obstacles,
in which many different activities can be carried out,
has been created

The imposing wall made of recycled
steel hides cupboards and doors that conceal
the residence's different services
in its structure

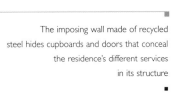

Architects: Mark Guard Architects

Photographers: Allan Mower, John Bennet

Location: London, UK

Completion date: 1998

Surface area: 185 m²

A WHITE CANVAS

As a result of the refurbishing work, this old warehouse has been converted into a large white space in which, just like on a white canvas, the occupier can express his or her personality in a way completely free from any form of conditioning. The starting point was a deteriorated 185-m² space situated on the fifth floor of an old warehouse building with a privileged location next to the River Thames. An irregular floor plan, a number of circular columns, beams and brick walls were all there was in the building at the beginning of the project.

In an intent to dissimulate the irregularity of the floor plan, and at the same time obtain as much free space as possible to dedicate to diverse activities, the construction of a 23-meter partition wall, which runs from the entrance door to the bedhead in the main bedroom, was planned. In addition to organizing the space, it accommodates all of the installations and separates the utility room, guestroom, kitchen and bathroom from the main area which, in this way, becomes the main feature of the residence.

As neutral a space as possible was desired. For this reason, it was decided to hide any type of reference to its industrial past by covering the walls, ceilings, floors and columns in the whitest of whites. The only elements that break the silence of this extensive luminous empty space are two steel rails that cross the entire width of the apartment over which two tables with metal structures slide. These tracks go through the partition wall, which crosses the residence lengthways, perpendicularly and creates a sort of visual cross that divides the space into four parts. Accompanying the dining table, another immortal creation of modern design is found: the sculptural chairs with steel mesh bodies designed by Harry Bertoia in the middle of the 20th century.

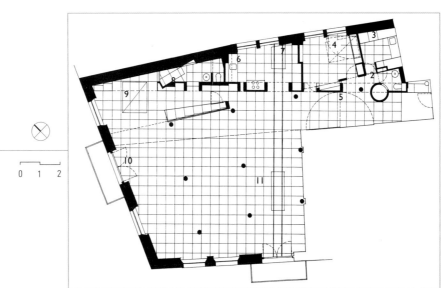

0 1 2

1. Entrance
2. Shower
3. Service room
4. Folding bed
5. Rotating door
6. Kitchen
7. Sliding metal table
8. Bathroom
9. Master bedroom
10. Balcony
11. Sliding glass table

An extensive empty space covered
in luminous white is the outstanding feature
of this loft. The bed located in the corner
can be isolated from the main area
by means of a four-meter-long
sliding door

All references to the industrial background
of this residence have been eliminated. All pipes and cables
being out of sight frees our overall perception of the space
from any distraction or «noise» that could possibly alter
the sensation of purity that it gives

■

Architect: JOAN BACH

Photographer: JORDI MIRALLES

Location: BARCELONA, SPAIN

Completion date: 2000

Surface area: 125 m²

LIVING AT FOUR HEIGHTS

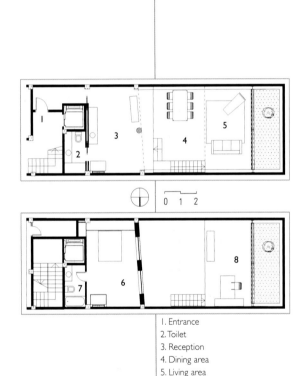

1. Entrance
2. Toilet
3. Reception
4. Dining area
5. Living area
6. Dormitorios
7. Bathroom
8. Study

The remodeling of this loft, located in the lower part of a building in the bustling district of Gracia, Barcelona, was based on the owner's desire that the space should fulfil the necessities of being both a residence and office at the same time. To be able to differentiate the diverse functions without the help of any enclosing systems, the architect decided to make use of the space's outstanding height and create a play on different levels.

Thanks to the four heights that the loft has been divided into, the different areas have all been perfectly delimited without any loss of visual connection from one to another. This division system has also helped make the most of the natural light that enters through the impressive glazed wall that opens onto an interior patio. If it were not for this system, the back areas of the loft would be rather dark as there is no entrance for natural light in that part. The skylights located over the office zone increase the intensity of natural illumination in addition to augmenting ventilation to the residence. This is achieved thanks to a mechanical system that allows the skylights to be opened.

On the ground floor, the entrance door is found, a discrete reception area that serves as much for the office as for the residence, and a toilet. Going down two steel steps we arrive at the level of the living dining area which has been decorated with very carefully selected furniture, such as the steel-structured chairs created by Mies van der Rohe, or the mythical chaise longue from Le Corbusier. From this level, a staircase, light in structure, leads to the office area. And the fourth and final level is accessed from the hall where a mechanical elevator, which goes to the bedroom and bathroom, is found. From this level, the entire loft can be seen as well as the patio that has been resolved with a certain inspiration in Zen.

The bedroom has been resolved with extreme simplicity.
A bed on wheels and a wardrobe lacquered in white,
which also serves as a bedhead, are the only decorative
elements found here. From the bed, the entire residence
can be appreciated thanks to the strip of transparent glass
situated at floor level

Architects: CHA & INNERHOFER ARCHITECTS

Collaborators: KAZ MORIHATA, ALI TURAN KOLUMAN, CHRISTOPHER MOON

Photographer: DAO-LOU ZHA

Location: NEW YORK, US

Completion date: 1998

Surface area: 372 m²

PLANES AND MASSES

1. Entrance
2. Dining area
3. Kitchen
4. Living dining area
5. Passage
6. Bedroom principal
7. Bathrooms

0   1   2

This 372-m² apartment in New York's Soho is the residence of a banker who desired a peaceful space in which to retreat from his busy daily routine and something that provided elegant surroundings for social meetings. As a result, the residence has been divided into two equal parts: one destined to socializing, which includes the kitchen, dining area and living area, and the other to a more private life in which the bathrooms, television room and bedroom are found. The two zones are separated by means of a partition made in cheery wood that can be moved over its own axis and into which a square of transparent glass has been inserted to maintain the visual continuity between the public and private zones, but without loss of privacy.

The construction can be defined as a play on planes and masses that emerge from within the space creating different ambiences and perspectives that produce movement and areas of visual interest. Another of the residence's special qualities is the way different materials and textures have been combined in the flooring. This enriches the visual perception of the whole in addition to delimiting the different areas. In the entrance, living area, passage and bedroom, the floor is in sycamore wood. The flooring in the television room – which has been slightly raised above the level of the floor in the rest of the apartment - is in walnut wood while for the kitchen and dining area, limestone, which unifies the two areas, has been chosen.

The linearity of the partitions and separating elements has been slightly broken by geometric gaps and openings which have been used as an aesthetic resource to introduce dynamism into the environment. In certain cases, the spaces resulting from this resource are used as functional elements such as shelves or small tables.

The kitchen furniture was designed
by the architects and combines
cherry wood with stainless steel.
As a result, this area, in which the same
materials and constructive concepts as
in the other zones have been used,
integrates perfectly into the overall
surroundings

■

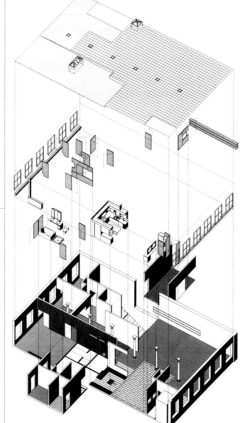

Axonometric perspective

The use of cherry wood in the decoration
of both the public and private zones
unifies the two areas. Partitions,
furniture and doors share the
textures and nobleness
of this material

Architects: OLLI SARLIN & MARJA SOPANEN

Photographer: ARNO DE LA CHAPELLE

Location: HELSINKI, FINLAND

Completion date: 1997

Surface area: 85 m²

BACK TO THE BEGINNING

This loft is an example of the rehabilitation of an old space. This is due to the fact that a large amount of the effort made in the course of the project was made to recover the characteristics of the original structure. The residence was originally the ground floor of a textile factory constructed in 1928 in the historic center of Helsinki and more recently recovered and converted into modern apartments.

The former owners had covered all of the beams with a false ceiling. Consequently, after tearing down all of the partition walls, the next step was to rediscover the beams by eliminating the false ceiling. The old brick walls were also restored and varnished pinewood flooring installed. The floor was previously treated with cellulose to reduce sound reverberations and to soften the noise made by walking. Between the floorboards and the walls along which the heating system was to be installed, a small gap was left for the pipes to be set into so as to ease any future repair work.

The result is an open L-shaped space with marked industrial aesthetics. Aesthetics reinforced by most of the furniture, such as the metal shelving, the kitchen furniture designed for industrial use or the large stainless steel storage cupboards recovered from a hospital, which also serve to separate ambiences. On the other hand, most of the furniture has wheels. This means that it can be redistributed in the residence with great ease. To make the most of the distribution, the bathroom and kitchen have been installed in the narrowest zone while the broadest space has been reserved for the living dining area and bedroom. The decorative elements have been reduced to an indispensable minimum and limited to those which have a determined function.

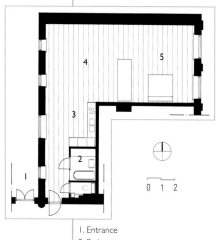

0 1 2

1. Entrance
2. Bathroom
3. Kitchen
4. Living area
5. Bedroom

To house the bathroom, a sort of plywood box
has been constructed that isolates it from the rest
of the space. This structure also contains the oven
and kitchen cupboards. The volume does not reach
the ceiling and, as a result, it manages to do away
with much of its visual weight as well providing
useful storage space

Most of the furniture used emphasizes the industrial aesthetics of the loft.
In many cases, it consists of pieces that have been recovered from
old industrial uses such as the stainless steel units in the kitchen or the cupboards
that came from a hospital

Architects: NON KITCH GROUP

Photographer: JAN VERLINDE

Location: OOSTDUINKERKE, BELGIUM

Completion date: 2000

Surface area: 180 m²

AN OVAL-SHAPED SPACE

The construction of this residence was based on the philosophy that its interiors would be in a complete union with its exterior surroundings. To achieve this, the traditional divisions between different spaces were done away with (by substituting partition walls with pillars) and an impressive glazed facade, 36m in perimeter, was installed. As a result, the occupants can enjoy the panoramic views from whatever place within their home.

The original oval-shaped floor plan imposes movement onto the space by introducing curves into its structure. The apartment has been divided into two halves. This has been done optically by using flexible elements such as the curtains that define the bedroom zone. The result is a layout that allows the exterior surroundings to be contemplated even from the entrance to the residence.

Around the front door, the only closed spaces within the apartment are located: the bathroom, on the left, a laundry room and a small storeroom on the right. The other areas respond to the desire of the project architects, Linda Arschoot and William Sweetlove, to create a large living area around which the rest of the spaces would be organized and which would all establish communication amongst themselves and, at the same time, a union between the interior and exterior in such a way that the changing light from the English Channel would be able to reach every corner of the loft.

The furnishing chosen has the quality of being simple, comfortable and, at the same time, the ability to transmit warmth. To heat this open space during the winter months, a heating system has been installed beneath the planks of the oak wood flooring.

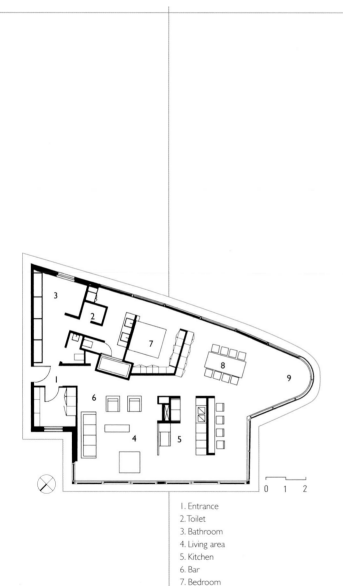

1. Entrance
2. Toilet
3. Bathroom
4. Living area
5. Kitchen
6. Bar
7. Bedroom
8. Dining area
9. Staircase

0 1 2

The furniture for the kitchen and bedroom along with the cupboards has all been designed by the architects themselves. The kitchen area has been confined within two walls of medium height, which house cupboards in the interior part, and has been raised over a low platform that visually sets it apart from the rest of the apartment

■

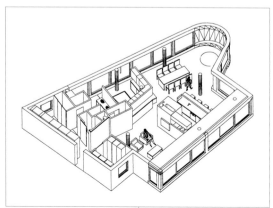

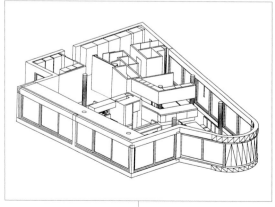

Perspectives of the residency

A metal spiral staircase situated at the vertex of the oval-shaped floor plan, leads to a terrace on the floor above. This has also been designed in such a way so as not to disturb the views or the free circulation of light within the apartment

The bedroom consists of something similar
to a box open at the sides and cut down the middle.
It can be separated from the rest of the loft
by light curtains that allow the light through.
From the bed, the landscape
can be enjoyed

■

Architects: Frank Lupo & Daniel Rowen

Photographer: Michael Moran

Location: New York, US

Completion date: 1995

Surface area: 150 m²

An expressive emptiness

This loft could have been inspired in the philosophy of Zen and the cult of nothingness as a means by which to free its environment of all the superfluous and to come to terms with, in this way, the essence of the most important things that remain. The result of the refurbishing work is a good example of fully-pledged minimalism as a philosophy of life which wishes to escape that materialist zeal to accumulate objects and to retain nothing more than what is truly indispensable. A surprising paradox considering that the residence is located in a central district of Manhattan.

The project has been based on the union of two traditionally distributed apartments that have been converted into one large white space. The result transmits a certain idea of abstraction, reinforced by the absence of furniture, the elimination of some windows and the incorporation of transparent glass screens that break the visual continuity and create a play on masses. Evidently, such an austere interior must have the owner's approval, as it is not everyone who could live in an environment so bare of ornamentation. In this particular case, it was the owner himself who asked for the elimination of all furnishings, as the changing light over the surfaces and its free flowing within the space was sufficient to satisfy his senses.

The partition walls do not quite reach the floor. This gives them a sensation of lightness as they appear to be floating. All of the functional elements, such as the rails for the sliding doors, the supports for the window blinds or the storage units in the bathroom, have been built-in so as to hide them from view.